Instant Hyper-V Server Virtualization Starter

An intuitive guide to learning Virtualization with Hyper-V

Vicente Rodriguez Eguibar

PUBLISHING

BIRMINGHAM - MUMBAI

Instant Hyper-V Server Virtualization Starter

First published: February 2013

Production Reference: 1190213

Published by Packt Publishing Ltd.
Livery Place
35 Livery Street
Birmingham B3 2PB, UK.

ISBN 978-1-78217-997-9

www.packtpub.com

Credits

Author

Vicente Rodriguez Eguibar

Reviewer

David Luu

Acquisition Editor

Kevin Colaco

Commissioning Editor

Ameya Sawant

Technical Editor

Dominic Pereira

Project Coordinator

Sneha Modi

Proofreader

Stephen Silk

Graphics

Melwyn D'sa

Production Coordinator

Melwyn D'sa

Cover Work

Melwyn D'sa

Cover Image

Valentina Dsilva

About the Author

Vicente Rodriguez Eguibar is the founder of Eguibar Information Technology S.L. Company, which is dedicated to providing IT consultancy and services, focusing on corporate directories, networking, virtualization, migration, and IT optimization. He has been a director of this company for the last four years, providing services and solutions to Fortune 500 international companies. He has traveled to several countries in Asia, Europe, and America supervising and managing projects for different companies.

His technical background started in 1993 as an IT trainer. He has also worked in many different positions as a system operator, technical project manager, and senior consultant for many international companies. Back in Mexico, where he was born, he was certified by Microsoft as a Product Specialist, being one of the first people to obtain this certification in Mexico.

At the beginning in México, he administered and managed computer systems for several industrial companies in the automotive sector. Following his performance in Mexico, he was required by the CIO office to design and manage the international communication network and corporate directory for their company. After managing this position for three years, he was hired by a German car manufacturing company to design the global corporate directory, being in this position for three years. When the German car manufacturing company sold the IT section to a German telecommunications company, Rodriguez Eguibar was appointed to design IT Architecture Infrastructures for external customer companies and government agencies. His last position before creating his own company was for an international call center corporation, where he was in charge of designing, deploying, and migrating to the corporate directory, messaging system, and virtualization strategy.

He was married in Mexico to Adriana Sainz 14 years ago; since 2001, he lives in Spain.

Thanks to my lovely wife Adriana, who has an inexhaustible patience born of love (and over 18 years of "dating"), even if I am using our family time for writing. To our parents, Angeles, Geo, Vicente, and Luis and our brothers Claudia and Luis A. because of their warm affection and close support, even though they are separated by a distance of 10,000 km. Special mention to Luis for his exhaustive comprehension of foreign languages, including the "IT for novices" language. And to all my friends and colleagues, who were always asking how I was doing. Thank you all!

About the Reviewer

David Luu is a Quality Assurance Engineer, Software Developer, Author, and Technical Writer.

His professional experience and interests include working with technologies such as virtualization, networking, Microsoft Windows, .NET, cloud computing, and more. By trade, David primarily tests software, products, and services, with an occasional side of software development, documentation review, and technical writing/editing tossed in.

He also participates in open source software, and has released a .NET library to facilitate programmatically managing Hyper-V virtual machines; this library can be found at http://code.google.com/p/robotframework-hypervlibrary/.

> Special thanks to Sneha Modi and Ameya Sawant of Packt Publishing for providing this opportunity for me to be a reviewer of this book.

www.packtpub.com

Support files, eBooks, discount offers and more

You might want to visit www.PacktPub.com for support files and downloads related to your book.

Did you know that Packt offers eBook versions of every book published, with PDF and ePub files available? You can upgrade to the eBook version at www.PacktPub.com and as a print book customer, you are entitled to a discount on the eBook copy. Get in touch with us at service@packtpub.com for more details.

At www.PacktPub.com, you can also read a collection of free technical articles, sign up for a range of free newsletters and receive exclusive discounts and offers on Packt books and eBooks.

packtLib.packtpub.com

Do you need instant solutions to your IT questions? PacktLib is Packt's online digital book library. Here, you can access, read and search across Packt's entire library of books.

Why Subscribe?

- Fully searchable across every book published by Packt
- Copy and paste, print and bookmark content
- On demand and accessible via web browser

Free Access for Packt account holders

If you have an account with Packt at www.PacktPub.com, you can use this to access PacktLib today and view nine entirely free books. Simply use your login credentials for immediate access.

Table of Contents

Instant Hyper-V Server Virtualization Starter   **1**

So, what is Microsoft © Hyper-V server 2008 R2?   **3**
Requirements and Installation   **6**
    Step 1 – MS Windows 2008 Server installed   6
    Step 2 – using the wizard   6
    Step 3 – Before you begin   7
    Step 4 – Select Server Roles   7
    Step 5 – Introduction to Hyper-V   8
    Step 6 – Create Virtual Networks   8
    Step 7 – Confirm Installation Selections   8
    Step 8 – Installation Results   9
    Step 9 – Installation Progress   9
    Step 10 – Installation Results   10
    And that's it!!   10
Quick start – creating a virtual machine in 3 steps   **11**
    Step 1 – deciding which virtual switch network you need   11
    Step 2 – configuring your virtual switch   12
    Step 3 – start creating your first virtual machine   13
Top features you need to know about   **20**
    Capacity planning   20
      CPU   20
      RAM   21
      Disk   21
      Network   22
    Virtual network   22
      The EXTERNAL network   22
      The INTERNAL ONLY network   23
      The PRIVATE VIRTUAL MACHINE network   24

Virtual disk and snapshot management 24
   The disks 24
   Snapshots 26
Making virtual machines portable 28
Providing access to Hyper-V 30
Reliability and fault tolerance 32
Integrating the virtual host 36
How much will it cost? 40
And that's it!! 42
People and places you should get to know **43**
Official sites 43
Articles and tutorials 43
Community 43
Blogs 44
Twitter 44

Instant Hyper-V Server Virtualization Starter

Welcome to the *Instant Hyper-V Server Virtualization Starter*.

This book has been specially created to provide you with all the information that you need to get set up with Microsoft © Hyper-V server 2008 R2. You will learn the basics of virtualization, get started with building your first virtual machine, and discover some tips and tricks for using Microsoft © Hyper-V server 2008 R2.

This document contains the following sections:

So, what is Microsoft © Hyper-V server 2008 R2? – find out what virtualization actually is, what you can do with it, and why it's so great.

Requirements and Installation – learn what is needed to install and how to install Hyper-V server with the minimum fuss and then configure it so that you can use it as soon as possible.

Quick start – create a virtual machine in 3 steps – this section will show you how to perform one of the core tasks of Microsoft © Hyper-V server 2008 R2; creating a virtual network so that your virtual machines can communicate between them and the world. Follow the given steps to create your own virtual infrastructure, which will be the basis of most of your work in Microsoft © Hyper-V server 2008 R2.

Top features you need to know about – here, you will learn all the necessary steps to get your virtualization infrastructure working, how to create a virtual machine, and make it more robust by anticipating any possible failures. You will also learn how to integrate this service into your existing network and how to measure and dimension it correctly. You will even learn to be aware on how to calculate the costs involved in your virtualization solution based on Microsoft © Hyper-V virtualization solution.

People and places you should get to know – this section provides you with many useful links to the project page and forums, as well as a number of helpful articles, tutorials, blogs, and the Twitter feeds of Microsoft © Hyper-V Server 2008 R2.

So, what is Microsoft © Hyper-V server 2008 R2?

Welcome to the world of virtualization. On the next pages we will explain in simple terms what virtualization is, where it comes from, and why this technology is amazing. So let's start.

The concept of virtualization is not really new; as a matter of fact it is in some ways an inheritance of the mainframe world. For those of you who don't know what a mainframe, is here is a short explanation: A mainframe is a huge computer that can have from several dozen up to hundreds of processors, tons of RAM, and enormous storage space. Think of it as the super computers that international banks are using, or car manufacturers, or even aerospace entities.

These monster computers have a "core" operating system (OS), which helps in creating a logical partition of the resources to assign it to a smaller OS. In other words, the full hardware power is somehow divided into smaller chunks that have a specific purpose. As you can imagine, there are not too many companies which can afford this kind of equipment, and this is one of the reasons why the small servers became so popular. You can learn more about mainframes on the Wikipedia page at `http://en.wikipedia.org/wiki/Mainframe_computer`.

Starting in the 80s, small servers (mainly based on Intel© and/or AMD© processors) became quite popular, and almost anybody could buy a simple server. But mid-sized companies began to increase the number of servers. In later years the power provided by new servers was enough to fulfill the most demanding applications, and guess what, even to support virtualization.

But you will be wondering, what is virtualization? Well the virtualization concept, even if a bit bizarre, is to work as a normal application to the host OS, asking for CPU, memory, disk, network, to name the main four subsystems, but the application is creating hardware, virtualized hardware of course, that can be used to install a brand new OS. In the diagram that follows, you can see a physical server, including CPU, RAM, disk, and network. This server needs an OS on top, and from there you can install and execute programs such as Internet browsers, databases, spreadsheets, and of course a virtualization software. This virtualization software behaves the same way as any other application-it sends a request to the OS for a file stored on the disk, access to a web page, more CPU time; so for the host OS, is a standard application that demands resources. But within the virtualization application (also known as **Hypervisor**), some virtual hardware is created, in other words, some fake hardware is presented at the top end of the program.

At this point we can start the OS setup on this virtual hardware, and the OS can recognize the hardware and use it as if it were real.

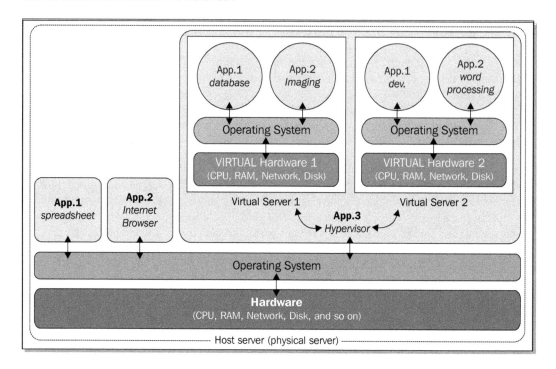

So coming back to the original idea, virtualization is a technique, based on software, to execute several servers and their corresponding OSes on the same physical hardware. Virtualization can be implemented on many architectures, such as IBM© mainframes, many distributions of Unix© and Linux, Windows©, Apple©, and so on.

We already mentioned that the virtualization is based on software, but there are two main kinds of software you can use to virtualize your servers. The first type of software is the one that behaves as any other application installed on the server and is also known as workstation or software-based virtualization. The second one is part of the kernel on the host OS, and is enabled as a service. This type of software is also called as hardware virtualization and it uses special CPU characteristics (as **Data Execution Prevention** or **Virtualization Support**), which we will discuss in the installation section. The main difference is the performance you can have when using either of the types. On the software/workstation virtualization, the request for hardware resources has to go from the application down to the OS into the kernel in order to get the resource. In the hardware solution, the virtualization software or hypervisor layer is built into the kernel and makes extensive usage of the CPU's virtualization capabilities, so the resource demand is faster and more reliable, as in Microsoft © Hyper-V Server 2008 R2.

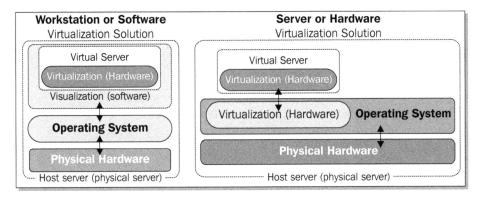

Requirements and Installation

Microsoft © Hyper-V server 2008 R2 provides hardware virtualization services, and it is configured as a role within the OS. The Windows 2008 editions that support the Hyper-V role are: **Standard, Enterprise,** and **Datacenter**. The **Foundation, Web,** and **Itanium** editions do not support this role. There is another edition, a free edition called Windows Hyper-V 2008 server R2, but it can ONLY be used for virtualization purposes. By the way, this version does not provide a Graphical User Interface (GUI).

In ten easy steps, you can install Microsoft © Hyper-V role and get it set up on your system.

Step 1 – MS Windows 2008 Server installed

Before you install Microsoft © Hyper-V role in your server, you will need to check that you have the right Windows 2008 version installed and that you meet all prerequisites, listed as follows (the official list can be found on Microsoft Knowledge base at `http://technet.microsoft.com/en-us/library/cc731898.aspx`):

✦ Review your hardware on the Microsoft Windows Server Catalog
   (`http://go.microsoft.com/fwlink/?LinkId=111228`)

✦ CPU x64. Windows 2008 Server R2 is only available for 64-bit architecture

✦ Hardware-assisted virtualization. Intel Virtualization Technology (Intel VT) or AMD Virtualization (AMD-V)

✦ Hardware-enforced **Data Execution Prevention** (**DEP**), enabling the Intel XD bit (execute disable bit) or AMD NX bit (no execute bit)

In order to configure HAV and DEP, a change in the computer BIOS has to be done, and a cold reboot (completely shut down the computer and start it again) has to be done. Each computer manufacturer may give a different name to each of these configurations. Please refer to your hardware manufacturer's help.

The setup and configuration of the Windows server is out of the scope of this book, but you can refer to the Microsoft TechNet site at `http://technet.microsoft.com/en-us/library/dd379511(v=ws.10).aspx` or a very good guide from our friends at Petri, `http://www.petri.co.il/how-to-install-windows-server-2008-step-by-step.htm`.

Step 2 – using the wizard

Starting with Windows 2008, Microsoft© includes a very good command-line interface (known as **PowerShell**), which can be used to do the same things as in the graphical interface, but because this is a Starter series book, this will be left for another work.

As mentioned before, we are about to install the Hyper-V role. To do this, we have to open the **Server Manager** console, select the **Roles** node on the left, and select **Add Roles** on the right, as shown here:

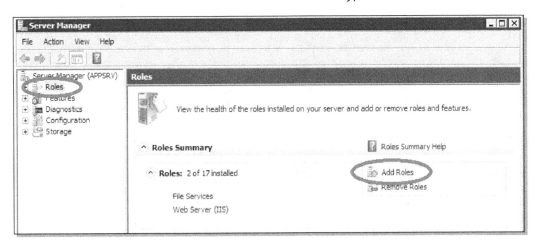

Step 3 – Before you begin

The first step of the wizard indicates the main propose of the wizard (adding roles) and it gives us some good practice. This step can be skipped by default by ticking the checkbox at the bottom.

Step 4 – Select Server Roles

In this step we can select which role or roles we want to install, in our case we will select the **Hyper-V** role. Note that some of the roles have to be installed separately. If you click on any role, the wizard will show a brief description on the right side of the wizard.

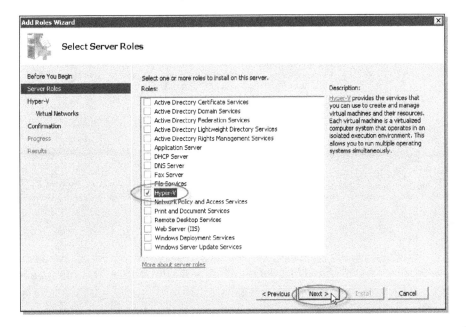

Step 5 – Introduction to Hyper-V

Here we can read a brief description of Hyper-V and what we can do with it. A couple of notes explain the network cards to include for virtualization and the management console to access virtualization services. Some interesting links that point us to the help sections are displayed as well. Feel free to click on those help links.

Step 6 – Create Virtual Networks

We will have a detailed discussion on the virtual network management in the *Quick start – Create a Virtual Machine in 8 steps* and *Top features you need to know about* sections. But when configuring the **Hyper-V** role, we have to choose the **Network Interface Card** (**NIC**) that will be used by our virtual machines. It is recommended to have at least two NICs, but depending on your hardware configuration, it can be at least one or as many as supported. When your hardware has more than two NICs, it is recommended to leave one NIC for host management (think of host as the physical server) and the rest of the NICs can be used to provide access to different network segments and to assign them through virtual switches (described in the following sections) to one or several virtual machines.

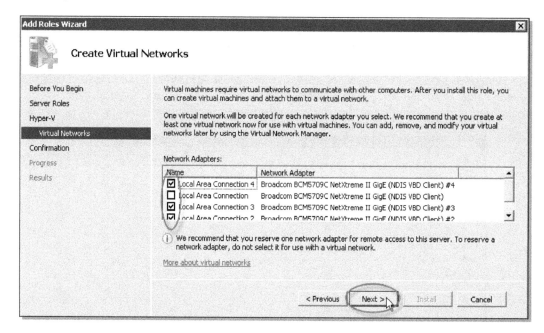

Step 7 – Confirm Installation Selections

A summary is displayed in this step, including the NICs to be used and a message indicating that the server may need to reboot in order to complete the installation. This information can be printed, e-mailed, or saved for further reference.

Step 8 – Installation Results

The setup process will start installing some components, but will show a warning indicating a reboot is needed. The reboot is needed to replace a set of components that are in use by the OS. We have to click on the **Close** button and a pop-up window asking if we want to reboot the server will appear. Click **Yes** in order to initiate the server reboot.

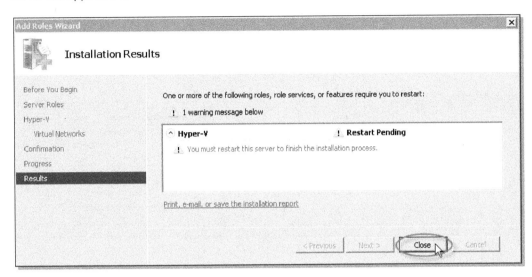

Step 9 – Installation Progress

After the reboot is completed, and we log in again with the same user, the installation will continue automatically, showing the progress of the task.

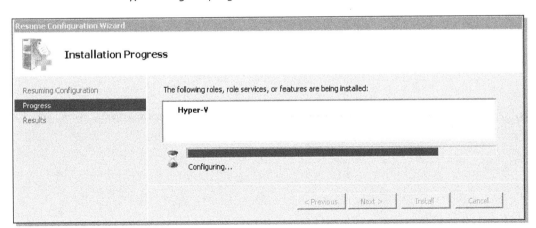

Step 10 – Installation Results

And now we have reached our goal: the green circle check saying **Installation Succeeded**. Congratulations, you already have enabled Hyper-V role on your server and now you can continue reading to create your virtual machines.

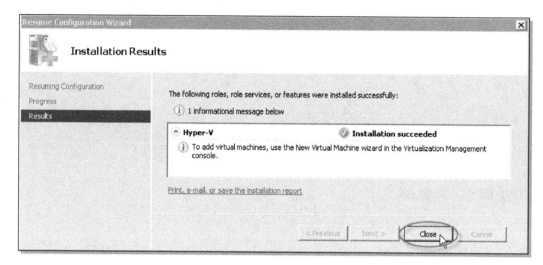

And that's it!!

At this point, you should have a working installation of Microsoft © Hyper-V server 2008 R2 with a **Hyper-V** role. Please feel free to play around and discover more about it.

Quick start – creating a virtual machine in 3 steps

Now that you have your hypervisor running, you are in shape to create your first virtual machine (VM). Having this role installed without virtual machines running on top is a bit useless. In this section you will learn how to create it. So let's get for it.

Step 1 – deciding which virtual switch network you need

Years ago (and don't think I'm too old!) personal computers were mainly standalone, they then slowly started to get connected between them, creating Local Area Connections (LAN). As the technology advanced, more ways to connect the devices appeared and the LANs got bigger. To control this growth, many network devices were introduced, as in the case of switches, and of course our virtual switches (or **vSwitch**).

For our virtual machines to have communication with others, we need at least 1 vSwitch configured. There are three ways to configure your vSwitch, but we are going to discuss this in detail later in the *Virtual Network* section. Now what we need is:

✦ At least one physical NIC connected to the network that you want to provide access to

✦ One "External" virtual switch configured on your Hyper-V server

You can configure as many vSwitches as you need, and bind each of them to the different NICs configured on Hyper-V. Remember how we configured the physical NICs earlier, in *Step 6 – Create Virtual Networks* of the previous section. These vSwitches can provide different isolation layers and segregated access to different network types. One limitation is that a physical NIC can only be assigned to a single virtual network or vSwitch.

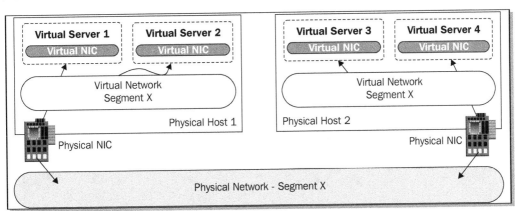

In this very first example, we will use the principal NIC that, hopefully, is giving us Internet access. This NIC will be part of the External vSwitch used by our just-about-to-be-created virtual machine. In simpler words: Physical NIC to vSwitch to your Virtual Machine.

Step 2 – configuring your virtual switch

To start configuring your first vSwitch, open the **Microsoft Management Console** (**MMC**) for Hyper-V by selecting **Start | Administrative Tools | Hyper-V Manager**. On the right-hand side of the console, select the **Virtual Network Manager** link. This will display a two-step wizard.

On the left pane, make sure **New Virtual Network** is selected. On the right pane **External** should be selected. Now we can use the **Add** button to add the vSwitch and configure it.

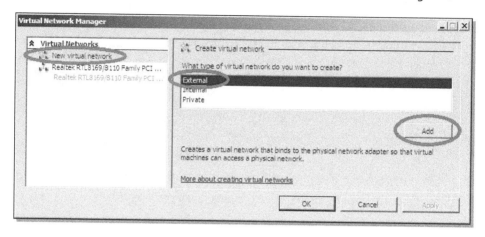

On this screen we should add a descriptive name for our network, in this case, **PUBLIC-EXTERNAL**. It is always recommended to add a description; it can be used as live documentation. Then **Connection Type** can be changed. As we are configuring an External network, we have to select the physical NIC that this virtual network will be using. The **Allow management operating system to share this network adapter** checkbox will share communication between Hyper-V and the host; if unchecked, communication is exclusively for Hyper-V purposes. If you only have a single physical NIC, this must be checked.

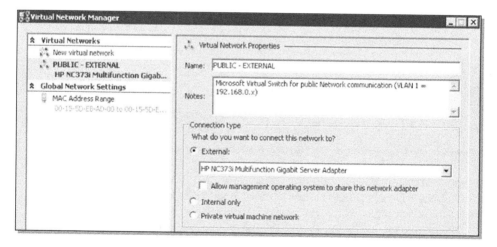

Step 3 – start creating your first virtual machine

Creating a virtual machine is a very straightforward process if we know what data to provide during creation. Here we will explain all the details needed to have a reliable configuration. We have to start the Hyper-V Manager console:

1. On the right side pane, click on the **New** menu and select **Virtual Machine** (from this menu we can create a virtual disk or virtual floppy as well).

2. The first wizard screen provides a basic info of what can be done. Note that if we click on **Finish**, a new virtual machine with default values will be created.

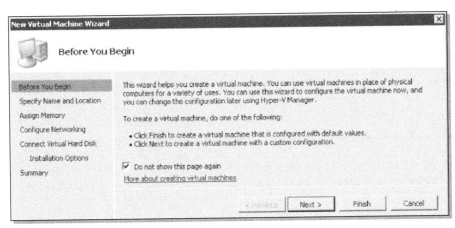

3. Think of a name for your virtual machine. This name will be used for some files and folders, and mainly to identify your machine. The same naming convention used for desktops, to ensure the uniqueness on the network, is recommended here. We can provide an alternate location to save this new virtual machine (by default the value stored on Hyper-V configuration will be used).

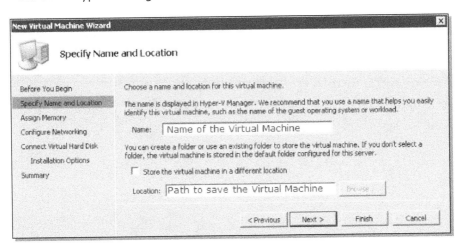

4. Assign the RAM memory your machine will use. This value is dependent on the physical RAM the host has, and we will discuss this topic in detail in the *Capacity Planning* section, but a value of either 1024 or 2048 would be fine to start with (1 GB or 2 GB respectively).

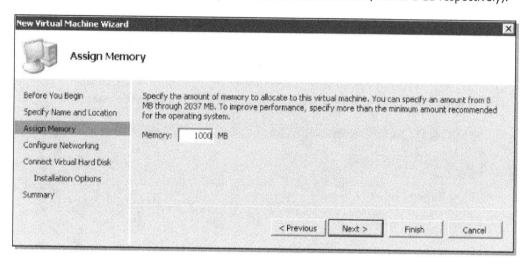

5. To configure the network, we just select the previously created vSwitch (the one called **PUBLIC-EXTERNAL**) from the combo box. Any created network will be automatically displayed here.

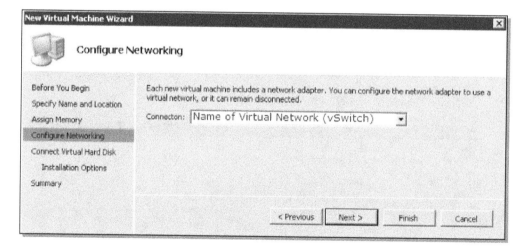

6. Create the virtual hard disk to use. The virtual disk has 3 main configurations: **Create, Use Existing,** and **Attach Later**. They are explained as follows:

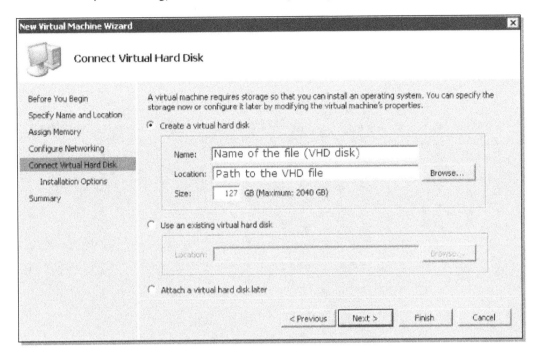

- ○ **Create a virtual hard disk**: As the name says, we will create a new disk, so we have to provide the name of the file-based virtual disk and the location where it is to be stored. If we don't provide a new location, the default will be used.

- ○ **Use an existing virtual hard disk**: Use this option whenever you already have a virtual hard disk to use. For example, when you already create a virtual machine with your favorite OS, with patches and additional software installed, you may "copy" this VHD file and use it as a template for any new virtual machine.

- ○ **Attach a virtual hard disk later**: In the event you don't have the disk at the moment of creating the virtual machine, you can skip this step and attach the disk later.

7. Installation options. In order to install the OS for our new virtual machine, we have to provide the media. We are presented with four Installation options: **Install later, from a boot CD/DVD, from a boot floppy disk,** or **from a network-based installation server.** These options, along with their descriptions, are shown as follows:

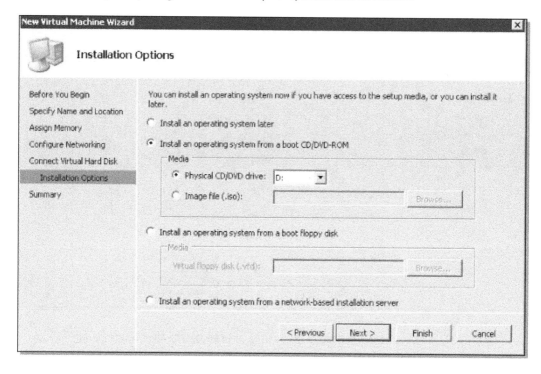

- ○ **Install an operating system later**: This is the most used option. When you finish configuring your virtual machine, on the property page, you can select this very same option to start installing the OS.
- ○ **Install an operating system from a boot CD/DVD-ROM**: You can choose the physical CD/DVD containing an OS disk to install or you can select an ISO file stored on your disk (a server path may also work as a **Universal Naming Convention (UNC)** path. For example, \\<server>\<folder>\file.ISO).
- ○ **Install an operating system from a boot floppy disk**: This option is not very useful anymore because we have CD/DVD bootable media, instead of a 1.44-MB floppy image, but if you do have such an image, let's say MS-DOS 6.22, you can install it on your virtual machine.

○ **Install an operating system from a network-based installation server**: These kinds of servers have one or several images ready to set up over a network. The configuration of this server is outside the scope of this book.

8. Review the configuration. In case you want to make any changes in the configuration, you can use the **Previous** button to go back and make those changes. If you like what you see, just click the **Finish** button. Note the checkbox, shown in the following screenshot, that will automatically start the virtual machine after it is created:

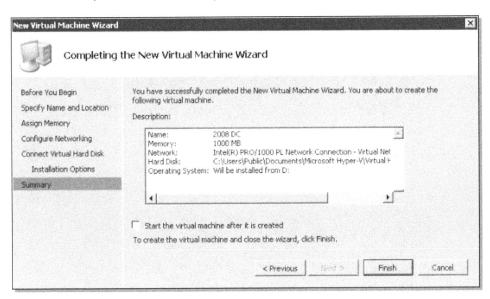

At this point you have a fully-functional virtual machine, and now you can start installing your favorite OS by booting from a CD/DVD (either a physical one or from an ISO file) or by using a previously installed and configured network-based install server. You can make modifications to your virtual machine from the **Hyper-V Manager** console or start it or stop it.

By selecting your virtual machine and right-clicking on it, you will be presented with a contextual menu for that machine. The most important settings right now are: **Connect, Settings,** and **Start** (or **Turn Off.../Shut Down...** if the machine is already running). The remaining settings will be discussed later in the sections that follow.

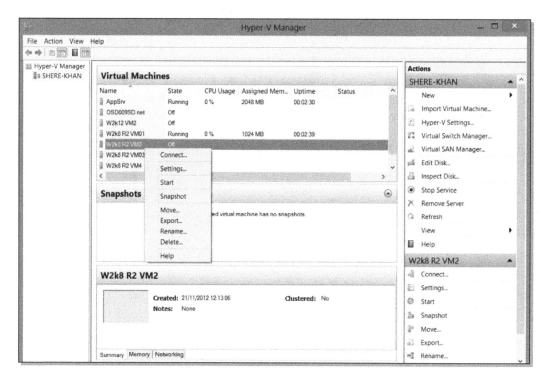

These important settings are explained as follows:

✦ **Connect**: It will link the virtual machine to the **Hyper-V management console**. If the VM is running with an OS installed, you can see and interact with it. If the machine is powered off, it will display something similar to the following screenshot:

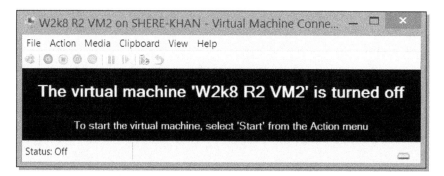

✦ **Settings**: Here you can change any configuration relative to the selected VM. In the next example, you can change the CD/DVD used by the virtual machine:

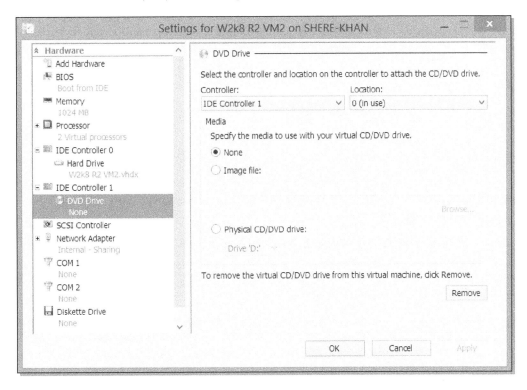

✦ **Start**: If the VM is powered off, you can start it independently whether you are connected to it or not.

✦ **Turn Off…/Shut Down…/Reset**: If the VM is running, you can decide to select **Turn Off…** (as when you press and hold the power button on your computer), or **Power Off…**, which will send a message to the OS ordering it to shut down. If the virtual machine is running, it can also be reset using **Reset** (awesome for people who have a crawling baby next to the computer who discovers such a wonderful button), restarting the virtual machine in a single step.

Top features you need to know about

Microsoft © Hyper-V server 2008 R2 provides many features, which we will try to cover in the following sections; but unfortunately there are many aspects in the virtualization world, so we will focus on the most important in order for us to get the most out of it and start using it right away.

Capacity planning

Wikipedia defines capacity planning (`http://en.wikipedia.org/wiki/Capacity_planning`) as follows:

> *The process of determining the production capacity needed by an organization to meet changing demands for its products.*

So is the total number of virtual machines, in our wonderful IT virtualization world, we can have with our current hardware.

As we defined in the *So, what is Microsoft © Hyper-V server 2008 R2?* section, a virtual machine is, among other things, a kind of partition or division of physical resources between the host server and the running virtual machines. Everything in this world has a limit, including virtual machines; our task is to identify that limit.

The first thing to bear in mind is that each virtual machine has to be dimensioned according to the role it is hosting, or the software running on it. In other words, if the VM is going to be a SQL server, we have to dimension it according to the database requirements in terms of CPU, RAM, disk, network, and so on. We should not treat the file server VM and a Microsoft Exchange Server 2010 VM in the same way. The four main subsystems to take care of are as follows:

CPU

Nowadays, CPUs can provide tons of power, which you can share between your VMs, but you still have to consider the number of running VMs and how CPU intensive those VMs are. If you plan to have a few VMs and the main purpose of have these is for lab testing, then a two-core CPU will do the trick, but if you have several VMs and those are CPU-intensive machines, then a four-core or six-core CPU must be used. For a good production environment, a two-socket server (server with two CPUs installed) will be more adequate. If you plan to virtualize your physical servers, it is recommended to gather the current CPU usage and take this value as an entry point for dimensioning your Hyper-V server.

The virtual machine will benefit from the number of virtual processors configured, having a limit of four per VM. You can find more details about this at Microsoft Technet (`http://technet.microsoft.com/en-us/library/cc794868(WS.10).aspx`).

RAM

The physically-installed RAM on the host server will mostly determine the number of VMs that can run simultaneously on the server. If we have 8 GB of physical RAM, it will be nearly impossible to execute two VMs of 4 GB RAM each. So we have to carefully plan the RAM distribution. As a rule of thumb we have to "reserve" at least 1 GB of RAM for the host (better if you assign 2 GB) and additional 32 MB for each virtual machine (again, better if we reserve 64 MB instead). The rest of the memory can then be assigned to the virtual machines.

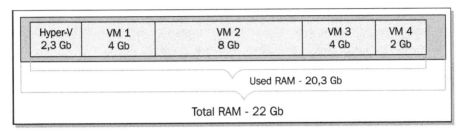

Similar to how we did in CPU monitoring, we will use the RAM-monitored data in order to plan our new virtual machine. You can't imagine how often RAM is underutilized in our machines. By digging into our monitoring data, we can define the initial RAM needed and the growth progression.

Windows 2008 Server R2 provides new functionality that helps improve the RAM usage. This is called **Dynamic Memory**, and the main task is to grant or retrieve memory from VMs depending on how the memory is used at that moment. In order to use Dynamic Memory, the guest OS has to support such a technology (for example, Win 2003 R2 Service Pack 2 or higher, Win Vista Service Pack 1 or higher, Win 7 Service Pack 1 or higher or Win 2008 R2 Service Pack 1 or higher), and the Hyper-V integration services.

Disk

This is the subsystem that will introduce the most bottlenecks into our virtualization strategy. All VMs will demand **IOps (Input/Output per second)** and each disk has a limited number of these IOps, so they will have to be shared between the VMs, the host OS, and any other service configured on it. There are some techniques (as array of disks/RAID, or network attached storage/NAS to mention some) that will overcome these bottlenecks. The second issue we can find is space storage. It is very easy to store several GB on disk, and if we multiply by the number of apps times the number of VMs, we can easily end up with terabytes of information. As a bottom line, we have to plan for good shared performance with adequate storage space.

Again, monitoring data can be your ally when you are planning the storage space. By knowing the maximum IOps, your infrastructure can plan the growth, and you can assign current services to the infrastructure without pain.

Network

When we are using a 100-megabit NIC in our desktop, it is very unlikely that we will find a bottleneck there; but if we run several VMs over that, we can run out of bandwidth very easily. When designing your Hyper-V solution, decide how many LAN segments you will need (we will talk about this a bit more in the next section), the current network speed of each section, how many VMs will use the mentioned section, and the bandwidth usage of each VM. Ideally, you will have monitoring data, which will help you design your solution, but it is always a good idea to have a gigabit network segment (or several depending on your needs) and having your server network cards with the latest technology, so it can help you optimize network usage (as it may be TCP Chimney Offload, Jumbo Frames, network MTU to mention some). The simplest way to check your network usage is by using the **Task Manager** graph.

Virtual network

We've been speaking a lot about vSwitches, but until now we have created just one external switch without knowing all the benefits of it, and when to use it. We already know that there are three types of network, so let's go into it. A vSwitch can only be bound to one physical network at a time, but a VM can have more than one virtual NIC associated to a different vSwitch. For example, we can have a VM with two virtual NICs, one external for internet access and the other one internal for monitoring. There are many more networking options you can configure on virtual networks, such as VLAN tags or the MAC address range to use or even the specific MAC address for a VM, but for now we will focus on the types of network available and what benefits each one will grant us.

The EXTERNAL network

It is called **EXTERNAL** because it gives the same functionality as if it were physically connected to the LAN segment. In other words, this type of vSwitch is like the one you are physically connected to, and it provides the same benefits. So if you are planning to have your VM participate in your LAN segment as if it were another physical server, then this is your option.

By using this type of network, we have the option to enable or disable the **Allow management operating system to share this network adapter** checkbox. In case we only have a single NIC, then we must enable this option, otherwise we won't be able to manage the host OS; but if we have more than one NIC (as is the case in many servers), we can assign one NIC for management purposes and the others for different LAN access.

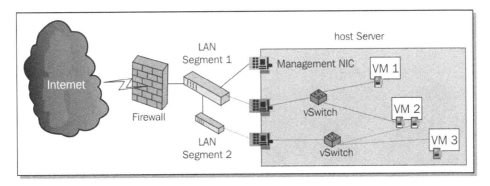

As you can see in the preceding diagram, the host server has three physical NICs connected to two different LAN segments, but one of the NICs is reserved for management purposes. The remaining two NICs are each bound to a vSwitch respectively (red vSwitch and green vSwitch respectively). The red VM1 and green VM3 are configured as a single vNIC to the corresponding vSwitch, but the VM2 has both vNICs, so it has access to both vSwitches. In topologies where we have a plain network with a single LAN segment, the idea of having several vSwitches may not make too much sense, but when we are dealing with much more complex topologies, then we have to accommodate our vSwitches, so that the right LAN segment access is available within the virtualization server.

The INTERNAL ONLY network

The internal network is for the VMs to communicate with each other and with the host. In other words, communication is possible between all VMs which use this switch, and the host. Because of the nature of these networks, you don't need to assign a physical NIC to it. These types of networks are used to provide a certain level of isolation between them; they are great for labs.

Access external networks using the INTERNAL vSwitch

Create the INTERNAL vSwitch, which will help facilitate the communication between VMs and the host, and because you can't assign a physical NIC to it, then we will enable **Internet Connection Sharing** on the physical NIC that we want to use as a gateway for communication (this is done by selecting the properties of the physical NIC and on the **Sharing** tab, select the **Allow other network users to connect through this computer's internet connection** checkbox and select the previously-created INTERNAL vSwitch there.

The physical NIC will act as a **Network Address Translator (NAT)** gateway and will act as DHCP for that vSwitch (In my laptop, I always get the 192.168.137.x IP address, and the default gateway and DNS is 192.168.137.1). You can modify the physical NIC routing table in order to access those VMs from the LAN.

In the following diagram, we can see the red vSwitch as an EXTERNAL vSwitch, and the green vSwitch as INTERNAL, but having the yellow physical NIC sharing the connection. Also the VMs are accessing their correspondingly-colored networks.

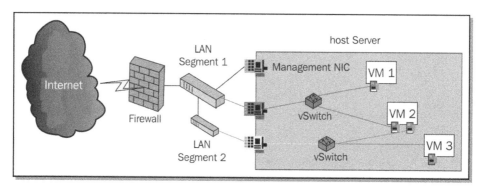

The PRIVATE VIRTUAL MACHINE network

Finally, the private VM network. This will only provide communication between the VMs. That is, only VMs using this vSwitch will have communication between them, not even with the host. This is the most isolated type of network, very good when all the servers and services live on the same vSwitch, but are completely isolated outside this boundary.

For more information, you can visit John Howard's blog at `http://blogs.technet.com/b/jhoward/archive/2008/06/17/hyper-v-what-are-the-uses-for-different-types-of-virtual-networks.aspx`.

Virtual disk and snapshot management

As with any other machine, a VM needs some storage space to function. The **Virtual Hard Drive** or **VHD** is the virtual piece that will grant such a storage space. Although VHD is not the only disk type, it is the most common and the only type that supports snapshots (which we will discuss right after finishing this topic).

The disks

There are four types of disks that we can use for our VMs, and we have to carefully plan in advance depending on what we want to achieve with each one of them.

- **Fixed**. This file file-based disk is created by using the maximum capacity, which is configured when is created. In other words, when we create the disk with a maximum size of 100 GB, Hyper-V will create a VHD file of 100 GB on the physical disk. And depending on the size and the disk performance, it can take a long time until the disk is created. These disks are quite portable and only depend on the copying process from one host server to another.

- **Dynamic**. In contrast to the fixed disk, this disk is created with a minimum space used, and will grow in size whenever new data is copied into it. These disks are almost instantaneously created. The disk will continue growing until it reaches the maximum configured size. This concept is also known as **thin provisioning**. These disks are the most flexible, because to copy or move them to another server, we only need to transfer the real data stored inside, which makes the overall process faster.

- **Differential**. We consider this as a child disk, because it depends on a parent or master disk. These kinds of disks are intended to store the new changes from the parent. In other words, you start with the master disk, and any write/delete operation that is done on the master is stored on the differential disk instead. These disks are automatically created when we create a snapshot on the VM (snapshot technology will be discussed in a while, be patient).

The fixed and the dynamic disks are the only disk types (having a differential disk as a consequence) that support snapshots. By default, these disks are created in `C:\Users\Public\Documents\Hyper-V\Virtual Hard Disks`, but you can define where to store the file when creating the disk; be sure to store these files in the correct physical disk to avoid future storage problems. Deciding to choose between fixed and dynamic disks is a matter of tradeoff, because the fixed disk will provide a slightly better performance, but it will use all the space configured.

On the other hand, the slightly slower dynamic disk will not consume all the configured space, but over time it will continue growing, and if we are not carefully monitoring our disks, it will eat up all the available space in the physical disk. So one option will take over all the disk space even if the virtual disk is not using it, and the other one will use it progressively with the risk of running out of space if we are not carefully monitoring it and taking action in advance.

VHD files can only be stored on NTFS volumes without enabling compression, and the maximum size is 2 Terabytes. When you create a new disk, the wizard will ask you what type of disk you want to create.

And the last consideration, but not the least important, is security. Because these types of disk are file-based, they can be copied into another disk, or another media as it can be an external USB disk. So protecting these files accordingly is a must in order to avoid unauthorized copying of data.

Pass-through. This is how it is called when the virtual machine is directly using a physical disk. These types of disk provide the best performance (very significant when comparing average reads and writes, but very little difference when comparing IOps), but as a tradeoff do not support snapshots and it is quite complicated to migrate or move them. As a matter of fact, it takes the same effort to move or copy these types of disks as a physical disk. It is a physical disk, but a VM is accessing it instead of the physical host.

You may be wondering why we want to use a pass-through disk if we have a fully-featured and a very portable VHD; well, in some cases we do not need such a functionality, and we can achieve portability by using different technologies. For example, it's recommended that our virtualized Active Directory Domain Controllers be installed in pass-through disks, because AD object replication can be severely damaged by a snapshot (as Microsoft recommends on this Tech Net article at `http://go.microsoft.com/fwlink/?LinkId=159631`). But as mentioned earlier, portability is almost eliminated from these kind of disks; well, not fully true. For example, if we use the pass-through disk as an iSCSI disk (we will discuss it further in the upcoming *Reliability and Fault Tolerance* section, but as a precis is a disk stored on a **Network Attached Storage (NAS)** by using a Block Access technology standard internet SCSI), which can be seamlessly disconnected from one server and connected to another without too much effort and with very little downtime, we can achieve a similar degree of portability.

Snapshots

Snapshots can be considered as a mechanism to travel back in time, IT time to be more precise. When a snapshot is taken, Hyper-V stores all the VM information and any change done after this point can be reverted. For example, we install Windows 7 with all its service packs and hot fixes, even install an antivirus and other software, and if we wish to "mark" this point in time, we take a snapshot. Later on we install all kinds of software and tools, but the first part of the installation of our Windows 7 still remains in the "parent" disk, so if we decide to go back to a previous state, we should only revert to the desired snapshot. Very simple, isn't it? But, how is this done? Well, it is done by using VHD files; the moment we take a snapshot, Hyper-V creates a differential disk (a file-based disk with an AVHD extension) where any change is written to.

So if we know what we are doing, taking a snapshot is only a matter of click and sing. But we do need to know what is going on when dealing with snapshots. As we already mentioned, when a snapshot is taken, the VHD file becomes a read-only parent, and a differential AVHD child file is created, so guess which file will start using the storage space? Correct, the differential file. Now we can start considering the implications of a snapshot:

✦ **Performance**: After the first snapshot is taken, two linked files, acting as a single virtual disk will exist, and each time a snapshot is taken, a new linked child of the child file will appear, leading to reduced disk performance.

✦ **Storage space**: Taking snapshots may rapidly consume all your hard drive space without any previous notice (unless you are a good admin and have set up monitoring alerts).

✦ **Recovering space from snapshots**: When you delete a snapshot (always from the Hyper-V management console, NEVER the file from explorer or cmd), storage space remains used until you shut down, turn off, or put the virtual machine into a saved state. At this point, Hyper-V will merge the file into the VHD and release the space used by the snapshot (differential file). This can be quite time consuming depending on the amount of data to merge.

+ Never take a snapshot when:
    ○ The service is time-based as can be Kerberos authentication, Active Directory, or any similar.
    ○ A potential performance problem exists (mainly on storage subsystems)
    ○ Running short on storage space
    ○ Alternative to a backup solution.

Now you should be asking, then why is this snapshot technology so marvelous if it has so many implications?

Well, it is a wonderful rollback tool for productive environments. Imagine you have your customer database server, and you need to apply a new software release on it, but you haven't got time to try it first on your Quality Assurance infrastructure (as a joke, but yes, we should not run without this), so you create a snapshot and proceed installing with the update. If everything went correctly, you just delete the snapshot and continue working as usual, but if the dam update breaks the critical customer database server, then you should not panic, and just revert to your snapshot; this will leave your server exactly as it was before the update.

You can use a snapshot as a dirty trick to change the storage used by some VMs (be careful when doing this, try it several times on your lab before messing with your servers).

It may also be used on your lab (I do have it like this in my laptop) to create a "master" disk with Windows 2008 that is ready to use, and any new server you create is using a differential disk, thereby saving space on your disk.

In the same way as we will not use a sport car as a truck, we will use also snapshots in the right scenario. Any snapshot taken of a certain VM will be created as a "tree" (similar to the tree of the file explorer) based on the time it was taken, so the latest one will be at the end of the tree and so on. Take special note that when deleting a higher node of the snapshot tree, all the children belonging to it will be deleted as well.

And finally the details. To take a snapshot, just click on the desired VM on the Hyper-V console, right-click on it and select **Snapshot**. This will generate a snapshot and it will be named `<Virtual Machine Name> - <Current Date and Time>`. By selecting **Apply,** the machine will be "traveling in time" and will end up exactly as it was when the selected snapshot was taken; all data after the snapshot date will be lost. To change the name of the snapshot, or to add a comment, select the **Rename** menu. As the name says, **Delete Snapshot** will delete the snapshot, in other words, there is no chance to return the VM to its previous state.

Once we delete the snapshot, file merging is pending until the VM is stopped, shut down, or in a saved state. And finally the **Delete Snapshot Subtree** option (these options are shown in the following screenshot) will delete the selected snapshot and the child hierarchy depending on it:

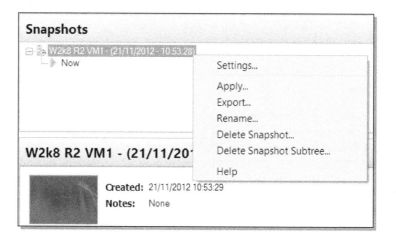

Making virtual machines portable

We are going to face situations where we will need to move our virtual machines from one server to another. In order to do this, we need to make our VM ready for the process. The first question we all have is, what will happen if we only copy the VHD file to the destination server? Well, this will retain all of the data stored in the disk, but we will be missing the VM configuration (VM name, CPU, RAM, NIC, and so on). Nothing to worry about, but additional work to perform because we will need to recreate the virtual machine.

One way or another, we have to copy the VHD file over to the destination server (remember that we can only do this if we have VHD files, either fixed, dynamic, or differential. It is not possible to do this task when using pass-through disks), but we want to save the task of recreating every single VM.

The best approach is to select **Export** from the virtual machine's contextual menu, and in the new window just provide the destination path to where we want to save it. But be aware that in order to export any VM, it has to be powered off or should be in a saved state. If the VM is running, there is no chance we can export it.

Exporting a VM is very straightforward, but what exactly happens in the background? We see almost nothing in the process, except for the **Status** column on the **Hyper-V Management Console,** which will be showing the export progress, until it reaches 100 percent and then disappears. This is very good because it means no errors were found and your export is complete. At this point we have an untouched VM ready to rock'n roll and a clone of it stored on the path you provided (don't forget to start your VM again). In this destination path we can find three folders (snapshot, virtual hard disk, and virtual machine) and an XML file having the configuration data. Now let's check the taxonomy of the export: the snapshot folder will have any snapshot that the VM had, if any existed; the virtual hard drive folder will have the VHD files used by the VM, exactly as they were in the original; and the virtual machine folder will have a quite long hexadecimal name with EXP extension. These wired files and folders are your VM once exported, including the friendly name you provided to the VM during its creation as a property inside the file. Hyper-V identifies each VM by using hexadecimal names (similar to the **Global Unique Identifier** or **GUID**) Note that this export is an exact clone of the original one, so importing and running this VM on the same LAN/Segment will create conflicts.

Importing a VM is also a very simple process. We select the **Import** menu from the right-hand side pane of the Hyper-V management console in the destination server. This will bring up the following window:

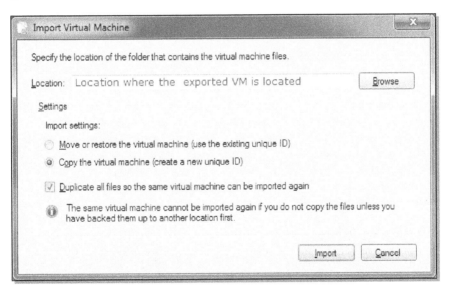

The import settings can be used to move or copy the selected virtual machine. If you are moving the VM, the unique identifier of the VM will be re-used (very good when the original VM will be deleted), or you can create a new ID by copying the VM. Unless you know exactly what are you doing, it is better and safer to select the copy option. The **Duplicate all files...** checkbox will make a copy of everything stored in the location provided, having all these files intact so we can re-import it again and again.

If this option is not selected, the current folder will be the folder used by the VM and it will not be possible to import it again without the need to export it once more. The taxonomy of the folder will remain almost the same, except for the EXP files, which will be changed to XML files and the `config.xml` file will be deleted.

Providing access to Hyper-V

We all know that in order to gain access to a server, we have the **RDP** protocol, which is better known as **Remote Desktop** (or **Terminal Services** admin mode). We just look for the **Remote Desktop** shortcut (or look for the `MSTSC.exe` file) and provide the server name or IP address and voila! We have access to the server (or any individual virtual machine). Even if RDP is a great technology, in many circumstances it is not the best tool to manage our servers. Connecting to host servers by using RDP, and then connecting to the VM through the Hyper-V management console (right-click the VM and select **Connect**) is not the best idea. Another example is when your host server is installed as Core (Windows 2008 Server R2 without graphical user interface) or when using the free Windows Hyper-V Server 2008 R2. Instead of opening RDP sessions, you would like to have the Hyper-V Management Console installed directly on your own local client and manage the host server and the VMs directly from there.

In order to remotely manage our server, we have to take care of the following:

+ Installing the management tools on your client
+ Enabling the corresponding rules in the Firewall (both host and client)
+ Checking if the host server and/or the client are in a workgroup environment

The first one is very simple, just download the **Remote Server Administrative Tools (RSAT)** corresponding to your OS, depending on whether you have Win Vista, Win 7, or Win 8 and the right architecture, either 32 bits or 64 bits (just go to the **Microsoft Download Center** web page and look for your corresponding download). Note that Microsoft does not provide RSAT tools for Windows XP; in this case you should buy a third-party tool. Once you have downloaded and installed the tool, you should go to the **Control Panel**, select **Programs | Features | Turn Windows Features On or Off**. From there you can select the tools you want to have available. Now we need to perform some additional steps before we can successfully execute the Hyper-V Management Console.

The next thing to take care is of having a TCP/UDP communication from and to the server. Older Windows versions had a very simple and easy-to-manage firewall, but Windows 2008 Server has a very complete firewall, which we should correctly configure in order to remotely manage our Hyper-V without losing security. We could run this configuration by using the Firewall GUI, but there is a simpler way, use the `NETSH.exe` command-line tool. Open a new command window (or cmd window) as an Administrator and enter the following:

```
netsh advfirewall firewall set rule group="Windows Management
Instrumentation (WMI)" new enable=yes
```

We should get an answer saying four rules were updated (three inbound and one outbound, but this may vary depending on which client OS you are using). We can confirm this by playing a little bit with the **Windows Firewall with Advanced Security** option in the **Windows Administrative Tools**. This command has to be executed on each of the Hyper-V servers and on any client you are planning to use for Hyper-V administration. There are some other firewall configurations you would like to implement. In case we haven't enabled the `Remote Desktop` rule, we should execute the following NETSH command from the command prompt:

```
netsh advfirewall firewall set rule group="Remote Desktop" new enable=yes
```

Or to enable all of the firewall rules for remote management of the server, use the following:

```
netsh advfirewall firewall set rule group="Remote Administration" new enable=yes
```

Or if you are planning to remotely manage the host server disk volumes by using the MMC, just execute the following:

```
Netsh advfirewall firewall set rule group="Remote Volume Management" new enable=yes
```

And last, but not least, we have to consider the domain membership (or the lack of it) of the computers running the Hyper-V role and the ones used to administer it. Here we can find the following four scenarios:

+ The Hyper-V host server and the client management computer belong to an Active Directory domain and are fully trusted

+ The Hyper-V host server is a domain member server, but the management computer is in a workgroup

+ The management computer is joined to a domain, but the Hyper-V host server is in a workgroup

+ Both the Hyper-V host server and the management client are in a workgroup

Following this order, the easiest and most secure setup is when both machines are joined to an Active Directory domain, and the preceding described configuration is considering this scenario.

John Howard, a Senior Program Manager in the Hyper-V team at Microsoft Corporation has created a very powerful tool (HVRemote, which can be found at `http://archive.msdn.microsoft.com/HVRemote`), which can help us to fully configure our server in a few steps for the mentioned scenarios. You can find his blog at `http://blogs.technet.com/b/jhoward/archive/2008/03/28/part-1-hyper-v-remote-management-you-do-not-have-the-requested-permission-to-complete-this-task-contact-the-administrator-of-the-authorization-policy-for-the-computer-computername.aspx`.

Reliability and fault tolerance

By placing all the eggs in the same basket, we want to be sure that the basket is protected. Now think that instead of eggs, we have virtual machines, and instead of the basket, we have a Hyper-V server. We require that this server is up and running most of the time, rendering into reliable virtual machines that can run for a long time.

For that reason we need a fault tolerant system, that is to say a whole system which is capable of running normally even if a fault or a failure arises. How can this be achieved? Well, just use more than one Hyper-V server. If a single Hyper-V server fails, all running VMs on it will fail, but if we have a couple of Hyper-V servers running hand in hand, then if the first one becomes unavailable, its twin brother will take care of the load. Simple, isn't it? It is, if it is correctly dimensioned and configured. This is called **Live Migration**.

In a previous section we discussed how to migrate a VM from one Hyper-V server to another, but using this import/export technique causes some downtime in our VMs. You can imagine how much time it will take to move all our machines in case a host server fails, and even worse, if the host server is dead, you can't export your machines at all. Well, this is one of the reasons we should create a **Cluster**.

As we already stated, a fault tolerant solution is basically to duplicate everything in the given solution. If a single hard disk may fail, then we configure additional disks (as it may be RAID 1 or RAID 5), if a NIC is prone to failure, then teaming two NICs may solve the problem. Of course, if a single server may fail (dragging with it all VMs on it), then the solution is to add another server; but here we face the problem of storage space; each disk can only be physically connected to one single data bus (consider this the cable, for simplicity), and the server must have its own disk in order to operate correctly. This can be done by using a single shared disk, as it may be a directly connected SCSI storage, a SAN (Storage Area Network connected by optical fiber), or the very popular NAS (Network Attached Storage) connected by NICs.

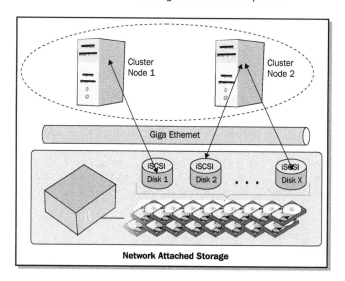

As we can see in the preceding diagram, the red circle has two servers; each is a node within the cluster. When you connect to this infrastructure, you don't even see the number of servers, because in a cluster there are shared resources such as the server name, IP address, and so on. So you connect to the first available physical server, and in the event of a failure, your session is automatically transferred to the next available physical server. Exactly the same happens at the server's backend. We can define certain resources as shared to the cluster's resources, and then the cluster can administer which physical server will use the resources. For example, consider the preceding diagram, there are several iSCSI targets (Internet SCSI targets) defined in the NAS, and the cluster is accessing those according to the active physical node of the cluster, thus making your service (in this case, your configured virtual machines) highly available. You can see the iSCSI FAQ on the Microsoft web site (`http://go.microsoft.com/fwlink/?LinkId=61375`).

In order to use a failover cluster solution, the hardware must be marked as *Certified for Windows Server 2008 R2* and it has to be identical (in some cases the solution may work with dissimilar hardware, but the maintenance, operation, capacity planning, to name some, will increase thus making the solution more expensive and more difficult to possess). Also the full solution has to successfully pass the **Hardware Configuration Wizard** when creating the cluster. The storage solution must be certified as well, and it has to be Windows Cluster compliant (mainly supporting the SCSI-3 Persistent Reservations specification), and is strongly recommended that you implement an isolated LAN exclusively for storage purposes. Remember that to have a fault tolerant solution, all infrastructure devices have to be duplicated, even networks. The configuration wizard will let us configure our cluster even if the network is not redundant, but it will display a warning notifying you of this point.

Ok, let's get to business. To configure a fault tolerant Hyper-V cluster, we need to use **Cluster Shared Volumes**, which, in simple terms, will let Hyper-V be a clustered service. As we are using a NAS, we have to configure both the ends—the iSCSI initiator (on the host server) and the iSCSI terminator (on the NAS). You can see this Microsoft Technet video at `http://technet.microsoft.com/en-us/video/how-to-setup-iscsi-on-windows-server-2008-11-mins.aspx` or read the Microsoft article for more information on how to configure iSCSI initiators at `http://technet.microsoft.com/en-us/library/ee338480(v=ws.10).aspx`. To configure the iSCSI terminator on the NAS, please refer to the NAS manufacturer's documentation. Apart from the iSCSI disk configuration we have for our virtual machines, we need to provide a **witness disk** (known in the past as **Quorum disk**). This disk (using 1 GB will do the trick) is used to orchestrate and synchronize our cluster.

Once we have our iSCSI disk configured and visible (you can check this by opening the **Computer Management** console and selecting **Disk Management**) in one of our servers, we can proceed to configure our cluster.

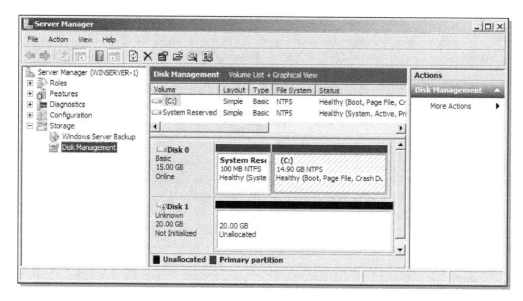

To install the **Failover Clustering** feature, we have to open the **Server Manager** console, select the **Roles** node on the left, then select **Add Roles**, and finally select the **Failover Clustering** role (this is very similar to the procedure we used when we installed the Hyper-V role in the *Requirements and Installation* section). We have to repeat this step for every node participating on the cluster.

At this point we should have both the Failover Clustering role and the Hyper-V role set up in the servers, so we can open the **Failover Cluster Manager** console from the **Administrative** tools and validate our configuration. Check that **Failover Cluster Manager** is selected and on the center pane, select **Validate Configuration** (a right-click can do the trick as well). Follow all the instructions and run all of the tests until no errors are shown. When this step is completed, we can proceed to create our cluster.

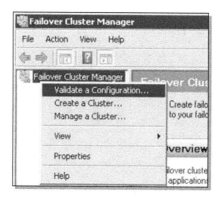

In the same **Failover Cluster Manager** console, in the center pane, select **Create a Cluster** (a right-click can do the trick as well). This wizard will ask you for the following:

+ All servers that will participate in the cluster (a maximum of 16 nodes and a minimum of 1, which is useless, so better go for two servers):

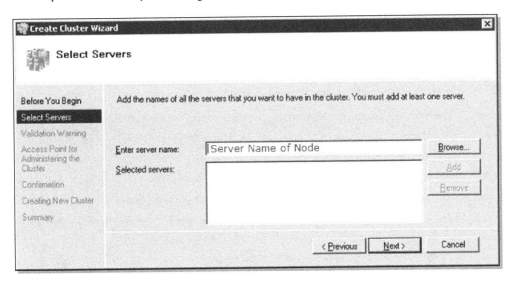

+ The name of the cluster (this name is how you will access the cluster and not the individual server names)
+ The IP configuration for the cluster (same as the previous point):

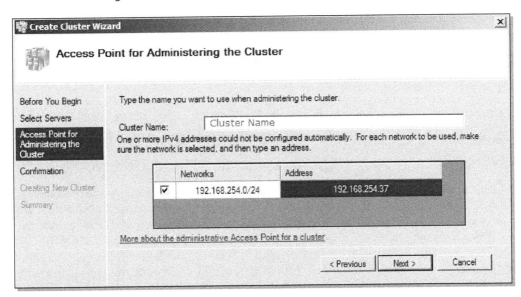

We still need to enable **Cluster Shared Volumes**. To do so, right-click the failover cluster, and then click **Enable Cluster Shared Volumes**. The **Enable Cluster Shared Volumes** dialog opens. Read and accept the terms and restrictions, and click **OK**. Then select **Cluster Shared Volumes** and under **Actions** (to the left), select **Add Storage** and select the disks (the iSCSI disks) we had previously configured.

Now the only thing we have left, is to make the VM highly available, which we created in the *Quick start – creating a virtual machine in 8 steps* section (or any other VMs that you have created or any new VM you want to create, be imaginative!). The OS in the virtual machine can failover to another node without almost no interruption. Note that the virtual machine cannot be running in order to make it highly available through the wizard.

1. In the **Failover Clustering Manager** console, expand the tree of the cluster we just created.

2. Select **Services and Applications**.

3. In the **Action** pane, select **Configure a Service or Application**.

4. In the **Select Service** or **Application** page, click **Virtual Machine** and then click **Next**.

5. In the **Select Virtual Machine** page, check the name of the virtual machine that you want to make highly available, and then click **Next**.

6. Confirm your selection and then click **Next** again.

7. The wizard will show a summary and the ability to check the report.

8. And finally, under **Services and Applications**, right-click the virtual machine and then click **Bring this service or application online**. This action will bring the virtual machine online and start it.

Integrating the virtual host

When we speak of integrating the virtual machine, what we mean is the fact that the host server is able to communicate directly to the virtual machine and the other way around. This internal communication has to be reliable, fast, and secure.

The hypervisor provides a special mechanism to facilitate this communication—the **Hyper-V VMBus**. As the name states, it is a dedicated communication bus between the parent partition and the child partition, or following the naming convention on this book, the host server and the virtual machines, which provides a high speed, point-to-point secured communication.

But what about the virtual machine? Well, as the VMBus is the Hyper-V part, we also need the client part. As you may expect, the component to facilitate such communication on the guest VM is a set of drives called **Integration Services**. In other words, a set of agents that is running inside our virtual machine, and communicates with the Hyper-V host in a secure and fast way. Once the OS in the virtual machine has installed these components, it becomes aware that it is a virtual partition and it can organize itself with the host beneath. With that said, you may be wondering, how is this going to be valuable for me? Well, consider a small example. If the tools are installed on the virtual machine, we could send a **Shut Down** message from the Hyper-V management console and the VM will shut down as if we were shutting it down from the desktop.

Now that we already know what the integration topic is about, we can talk about the two types of device drivers that Hyper-V provides—**emulated** and **synthetic**. As the name suggests, the emulated drivers are a very basic way of providing the service, in other words, they translate every request and move it through the VMBus until it reaches the hypervisor. The synthetic drivers do not have to perform any translation; they just act as the main gate to the VMBus until reaching the physical device on the host.

Before you ask, the emulated drivers exist to provide basic functionalities to every guest OS installed on the VM. In the initial setup stage of our VM, we do need some kind of device driver (as it may be display or network). You can think of emulated drivers as those cheap flip-flops that you can find almost anywhere at the beach. Those flip-flops are neither comfortable nor fancy (they don't even last long), but they will fit almost everybody thereby fulfilling their goal. Of course you want to change from using such an uncomfortable flip-flop to a more comfortable shoe, which fits perfectly to your feet, looks nice, and can even help you run with it. Well, think of that shoe as a synthetic drive.

As you may have already guessed, synthetic device drivers are not available for all OSes, but are only available for a more select group. Linux fans, don't worry, there are synthetic drivers for some of the most common distributions. The drivers for Linux can be downloaded from `http://www.microsoft.com/en-us/download/details.aspx?id=11674` and are intended for Red Hat Enterprise, CentOS, and SUSE Linux Enterprise. For a complete list of supported OSes (Linux and Microsoft), you can visit the Microsoft Technet site at `http://technet.microsoft.com/en-us/library/cc794868(v=ws.10).aspx`.

We are just one topic away from the installation of these drivers. But first we will describe in more detail what these drivers do:

✦ **VM connection enhancements**. If we connect to a machine without integration services, the mouse pointer will get trapped inside the VM, and we will have to use a key combination (by default *Ctrl + Alt +* left arrow) to release it. This enhancement will make the VM window behave as any other window.

✦ **Drivers with Hyper-V knowledge**: Remember the synthetic drivers. This is another name for them.

✦ **Time Synchronization service**: A mechanism to maintain time synchronization between the host and the guest. Because the guest has no BIOS battery, it uses the host clock to synchronize.

✦ **Heartbeat service**: The host sends heartbeat messages at regular intervals, waiting for a heartbeat answer from the guest VM. If any of these messages are not answered, then Hyper-V considers that virtual machine as having a problem and logs any such as an error.

✦ **Shut down service**: As mentioned earlier, a graceful shutdown of the VM without the need to log in and manually shut it down.

✦ **Volume Shadow-Copy requestor**: Provides an interface to the **Volume Shadow Copy** or **VSC** service in order to create shadow copies of the volume, but only when the OS supports it.

✦ **Key/Value Pair Exchange**: A set of registry keys used by the VM and the host to identify and obtain information. The host can directly access and modify such keys. You can see these values in the Hyper-V management console (in the VM properties).

The Integration drivers are fully supported on the following OSes. For other OSes not mentioned here, not all services and/or features may be available:

Operating system	Supported services
Windows Server 2008 SP1 and Windows Server 2003 SP2 32-bit and 64-bit versions.	Time Synchronization, Heartbeat, Shutdown, Key/Value Pair Exchange, VSS
Windows Vista SP1 and Windows 7 SP1 32 and 64 bit versions.	Time Synchronization, Heartbeat, Shutdown, Key/Value Pair Exchange, VSS
Windows 2000 Server and Advanced Server SP4	Time Synchronization, Heartbeat, Shutdown, Key/Value Pair Exchange
Windows XP SP2/SP3 32 and 64 bit versions.	Time Synchronization, Heartbeat, Shutdown, Key/Value Pair Exchange

Now the main dish. Installing Integration services is quite simple. The VM has to be running, and we have to connect to it using the **Connect...** option from the **Hyper-V Manager** console. From there we have to select the **Action** menu and select **Insert Integration Services Setup Disk**, as shown in the following screenshot:

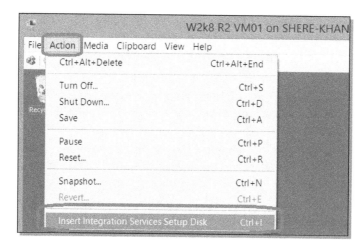

Depending on whether the CD-ROM autoplay feature is enabled or not, you may get a pop-up window asking to execute the inserted media. If you do, select the install option. If autoplay is not enabled, browse your CD-ROM and manually execute the **Integration Services** setup file.

A progress window will show how the components being installed on the virtual machine. Once finished, it will show a window asking for a reboot to complete the operation, as shown here:

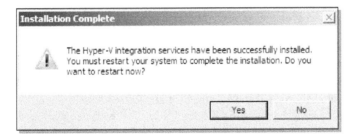

After the virtual machine is rebooted, the drivers will start working and your machines (both the hypervisor and the virtual) will be integrated. To review the configuration or to make changes, we can see the **Services** option from **Control Panel** on the virtual machine.

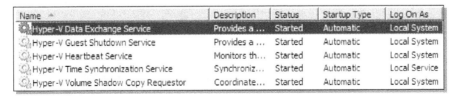

Or from the **Hyper-V Manager** console, select the corresponding virtual machine, right-click on it and select **Settings...** on the right pane of the settings window, click on **Integration Services**.

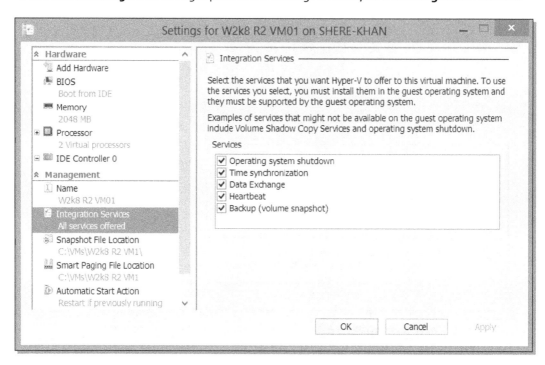

How much will it cost?

By now you should have a clear idea of what virtualization is, why it's so popular, and many other nice features. But we live in a business world, and because of this we will be facing the moment when we are asked: how much is this going to cost? And if you are like me, preferring nice toys such as Hyper-V rather than playing with numbers and ROI calculations, you will try to avoid it. Sorry to say it, but any effective economic quote must start with people like us.

The **Return of Investment** (**ROI**) is in simple terms the profit we will make in certain periods related to the investment. Nowadays everybody wants to increase their ROI. This can be accomplished by introducing new technologies that make our life easier, by consolidating and reducing the infrastructure, or by simplifying the administration. Our challenge is to identify such investments and treat these numbers, so that we can present the ROI in different ways. Don't misunderstand me when I say treat those numbers, it's not a manipulation but a different understanding instead. We have the hard costs of our solution, and understand that the hard costs are hardware or software or anything that is easily accounted for, most of time by a single invoice. And then you have the infamous soft costs, which can be as simple as how many watts my server is using or as complicated as the percentage of operational cost (including help desk) that one single window's server uses.

There are many ways to calculate these things, but the procedure used may vary from company A to company B, because what it is important to A may not be useful to B and vice versa. You may be wondering, how should I calculate this? And how do I know if it is correct or not? Well, if you do it and whoever you report to understands and agrees on it, then it is correct. As you already figured out, in this section we are not going to go through this exercise, but instead give you a good baseline to start this task according to your own environment.

Let's start with the calculations. Hardware investment. In a typical (or call it physical) environment, you buy a CPU (to name one component) that is capable of delivering its power to the application on top, even if the application is in a slow state. Simply put, you bought a CPU that is being utilized on an average of 25 percent (or 35 percent or any other percentage low below the full utilization of the chip). By virtualizing, you may share the CPU load over the configured virtual machines, making for a much better utilization; the challenge is to assign an economic value to both scenarios and compare them. The hardware cost is not assigned to a single server (like if you have your dedicated database server for HR), but to each single virtual machine running on that hardware.

Continuing with the calculations, we have to take care of housing (that is the required facilities to have the servers, the computer room, the air conditioner to maintain our devices, the electricity used, the cabling, and so on), which can be very simple in case we have a single closet or very complex if we have a dedicated room. As a rule of thumb, we will consider the devices + setup cost + running expenses divided between every service provided. As we are speaking about virtualization, a single server may host several virtual machines, so the calculated cost will decrease where we have more VMs, even if the host servers are bigger and more powerful (and likely more expensive).

Then we have the software cost. Traditionally, we need one OS license per physical server, or 100 in case we have 100 servers, but Microsoft has developed a very interesting licensing scheme.

In case we are deploying any other virtualization technology, we have to buy a license per each VM, no matter what. If we are planning to deploy Windows Hyper-V server 2008 (which by the way is a free license), we still need to have an OS license per VM. But for the remaining three versions of Windows 2008 Server (Standard, Enterprise, and Datacenter), we have a nice deal, while they are only installed and dedicated as Hyper-V hosts (yes, unfortunately we cannot even install a simple DNS on the host).

For the Standard version, we have included one OS license for a VM (say we have one for the host OS plus one for a VM); for the Enterprise we have four OS licenses for VMs (again one for the host plus four for the VMs), and for the Datacenter... mmm, I even get nervous... we have unlimited licenses (well, this is a lie, because by design we have a limit of 384 VMs per node).

The bottom line is that choosing the wrong brand will bring no savings; choosing the right brand and the right version will lower down the licensing cost significantly (Hyper-V free plus 30 VMs at the cost of, let's say $200, is a total of $6000, but Datacenter plus 200 VMs is only the cost of Datacenter, even if this is $5000).

Dealing with licenses is always a bit of chaos, so it is strongly recommended to call your local Microsoft representative, who will be pleased to help you in your licensing journey.

And last but not least (and the biggest cost within our IT service) - the manpower. Imagine you and your colleagues having to visit the server on the second floor to reboot a device, and then go running to the sixteen floor because the server is not accessible by network. With our new Hyper-V infrastructure we will not face this (or if we do, we just have to run to a single place where the servers reside) because of the consolidated state of our machines. We will be optimizing our IT support even if we add more VMs.

Don't trust my own calculations, or even the Microsoft ones which claim that their solution is six times cheaper than their competitors. Take a pen and a piece of paper and create your own number, I'm completely sure you will love the final result, and so will your boss!

And that's it!!

By this point, you should have a fully working virtual machine running on Microsoft © Hyper-V server 2008 R2.

People and places you should get to know

If you need help with Microsoft © Hyper-V server 2008 R2, here are some people and places which will prove invaluable:

Official Sites

+ **Homepage**: http://technet.microsoft.com/en-us/windowsserver/bb310558.aspx

+ **Manual and documentation**: http://technet.microsoft.com/en-us/library/cc753637(v=ws.10).aspx

+ **Wiki**: http://en.wikipedia.org/wiki/Hyper-V

Articles and Tutorials

+ **Mike Nail's video**: Virtualization on Windows Servers. Very nice if you have a spare hour! http://technet.microsoft.com/en-us/video/hh780712

+ **Installing Hyper-V on Windows Server 2008 R2 from Daniel Petri**: http://www.petri.co.il/installing-hyper-v-on-windows-server-2008-r2.htm

+ **Installing Linux Fedora Core 8 on Hyper-V**: http://blogs.msdn.com/b/virtual_pc_guy/archive/2007/12/31/installing-fedora-core-8-on-hyper-v.aspx

+ **Technet Virtual LABs**: http://technet.microsoft.com/en-US/windowsserver/bb512925.aspx

Community

+ **Official forums**: http://social.technet.microsoft.com/Forums/en-US/winserverhyperv/threads

+ **More official sites and forums**:

    ° **Hyper-V FAQ**: http://technet.microsoft.com/en-us/library/dd744892(v=ws.10).aspx

    ° **Hyper-V Virtual Machine Snapshots FAQ**: http://technet.microsoft.com/en-us/library/dd560637(v=ws.10).aspx

    ° **Hyper-V Live Migration FAQ**: http://technet.microsoft.com/en-us/library/ff715313(v=ws.10).aspx

Blogs

✦ Ben Armstrong, Hyper-V Program Manager is The Virtual PC Guy: `http://blogs.msdn.com/b/virtual_pc_guy/`

✦ John Howard, Senior Program Manager in the Hyper-V team: `http://blogs.technet.com/b/jhoward/`

✦ Tony Soper's blog: `http://blogs.technet.com/b/tonyso/`

✦ Martin McClean's ThePosterGuy blog: `http://blogs.technet.com/b/theposterguy/`

✦ Hyper-V Community Blog: `http://hyper-v.nu/`

Twitter

✦ Follow Ben Armstrong—AKA Virtual PC Guy—Senior Program Manager on the core virtualization team at Microsoft: `https://twitter.com/VirtualPCGuy`

✦ Tony Soper, a Microsoft PM Windows Server at `https://twitter.com/tony_soper`

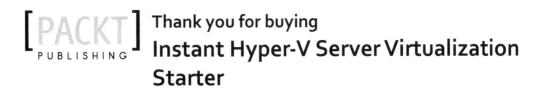

Thank you for buying
Instant Hyper-V Server Virtualization Starter

About Packt Publishing

Packt, pronounced 'packed', published its first book "*Mastering phpMyAdmin for Effective MySQL Management*" in April 2004 and subsequently continued to specialize in publishing highly focused books on specific technologies and solutions.

Our books and publications share the experiences of your fellow IT professionals in adapting and customizing today's systems, applications, and frameworks. Our solution based books give you the knowledge and power to customize the software and technologies you're using to get the job done. Packt books are more specific and less general than the IT books you have seen in the past. Our unique business model allows us to bring you more focused information, giving you more of what you need to know, and less of what you don't.

Packt is a modern, yet unique publishing company, which focuses on producing quality, cutting-edge books for communities of developers, administrators, and newbies alike. For more information, please visit our website: www.packtpub.com.

Writing for Packt

We welcome all inquiries from people who are interested in authoring. Book proposals should be sent to author@packtpub.com. If your book idea is still at an early stage and you would like to discuss it first before writing a formal book proposal, contact us; one of our commissioning editors will get in touch with you.

We're not just looking for published authors; if you have strong technical skills but no writing experience, our experienced editors can help you develop a writing career, or simply get some additional reward for your expertise.

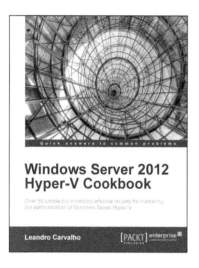

Windows Server 2012 Hyper-V Cookbook

ISBN: 978-1-84968-442-2   Paperback: 304 pages

Over 50 simply but incredibly effective recipes for mastering the administration of Windows Server Hyper-V

1. Take advantage of numerous Hyper-V best practices for administrators

2. Get to grips with migrating virtual machines between servers and old Hyper-V versions, automating tasks with PowerShell, providing a High Availability and Disaster Recovery environment, and much more

3. A practical Cookbook bursting with essential recipes

Windows Server 2012 Hyper-V: Deploying the Hyper-V Enterprise Server Virtualization Platform

ISBN: 978-1-84968-834-5   Paperback: 450 pages

Building a Hyper-V infrastructure with secured multi-tenancy, flexible infrastructure, scalability, and high availability

1. A complete step-by-step Hyper-V deployment guide, covering all Hyper-V features for configuration and management best practices

2. Understand multi-tenancy, flexible architecture, scalability, and high availability features of new Windows Server 2012 Hyper-V

3. Learn Hyper-V Replica, Hyper-V Extensible Virtual Switch, Virtual Machine Migration, Hyper-V Storage, Hyper-V Failover Clustering, and also System Center VMM and DPM for management, backup, and recovery

Please check **www.PacktPub.com** for information on our titles

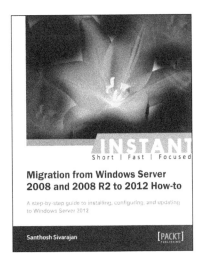

Instant Migration from Windows Server 2008 and 2008 R2 to 2012 How-to

ISBN: 978-1-84968-744-7

A step-by-step guide to installing, configuring, and updating to Windows Server 2012

1. Learn something new in an Instant! A short, fast, focused guide delivering immediate results.

2. Install and configure Windows Server 2012 and upgrade Active Directory

3. Decommission old servers and convert your environment into the Windows Server 2012 native environment

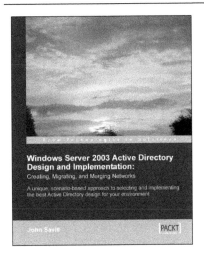

Windows Server 2003 Active Directory Design and Implementation: Creating, Migrating, and Merging Networks

ISBN: 978-1-90481-108-4   Paperback: 372 pages

A unique, scenario-based approach to selecting and implementing the best Active Directory design for your environment Understand the principles of Active Directory design

1. Create new networks or evolve existing Active Directory installations

2. Create the best Active Directory design for a broad range of business environments

3. Implement your Active Directory designs

Please check **www.PacktPub.com** for information on our titles